I0479805

the Metal Tiers of Insurance: a Choice for America

for my parents

Choosing between bronze, silver, gold and platinum plans seems simple, but reveals a more challenging choice and not so obvious solution. Understand not how you can make this decision for yourself this coming Open Enrollment...and whether this tiered system of insurance truly fulfills the intentions of the American Affordable Care Act.

Table of Contents

What are the Metal Tiers?

What are the different metal tiers in insurance?

The metal tiers in health insurance refer to the levels of coverage that are offered by health insurance plans. The different metal tiers in insurance are:

Bronze

This plan has the lowest monthly premium but the highest out-of-pocket costs. On average, a bronze plan pays 60% of the covered medical expenses, and the remaining 40% is paid by the policyholder.

Silver

This plan has a moderate monthly premium and a lower out-of-pocket cost compared to the bronze plan. On average, a silver plan pays 70% of the covered medical expenses, and the remaining 30% is paid by the policyholder.

Gold

This plan has a higher monthly premium but a lower out-of-pocket cost compared to the silver plan. On average, a gold plan pays 80% of the covered medical expenses, and the remaining 20% is paid by the policyholder.

Platinum

This plan has the highest monthly premium but the lowest out-of-pocket cost. On average, a platinum plan pays 90% of the covered medical expenses, and the remaining 10% is paid by the policyholder.

How to Choose

It's important to note that these percentages are averages and may vary by plan and by state.

The metal tier you choose will depend on your budget, health needs, and the amount of risk you're willing to take on in terms of out-of-pocket costs.

As you can see, a lower premium corresponds to a higher deductible: someone who doesn't use insurance much should select a policy that has this combination because they would be paying for more insurance than they would be using.

Saving the difference in premium from a low deductible plan, they would be able to afford a medical emergency if it did happen, and come out ahead! ...if they save the difference and not just spend it.

Someone expecting a large medical bill, such as for surgery, pregnancy, or who has a chronic disease with lots of doctor appointments and medicine would benefit from the lower deductible more than they are paying premium for.

Do Metal Plans Actually Help American Consumers?

The Affordable Care Act set out to standardize small-group and individual health insurance policies by creating a "metal" ranking for policies, with each level based on consumer value received.

The idea was to standardize insurance products to make the decision between them easier: it could be understood at a glance that a bronze plan had a higher out of pocket cost and a lower premium than a gold plan.

However, according to the Urban Institute's study *Marketplace Coverage Enrollment by Metal Tier, 2016–18: Trends in States Using the Healthcare.gov Enrollment Platform* (Wengle and Blumberg, 2020), "shifts from silver- to bronze-tier coverage pose risks for consumers. Specifically, bronze plans' low- or no-cost premiums are hard to resist for increasing numbers of people struggling to afford needed health care...Shifting to bronze coverage could be detrimental for enrollees' finances and health statuses. For example, an individual with an income of 175 percent of the Federal Poverty Level could have faced an out-of-pocket maximum of $7,350 in a bronze plan, as opposed to $1,950 in a silver cost-sharing reduction plan. Even people who have somewhat higher incomes and are ineligible for cost-sharing subsidies may have made potentially detrimental decisions because they did not understand the trade-offs between lower premiums and higher out-of-pocket costs. Such trade-offs will always be greatest for those with the greatest health care needs."

According to the Kaiser Family Foundation's study, "Marketplace Plan Selections by Metal Level" (2023) 32% of Americans over all selected a bronze level plan, 54% selected a silver level plan, 12% chose gold, 1% chose platinum, and less than 1% chose a catastrophic plan in 2022.

4 States have more than 50% enrollment in bronze plans: Nebraska, Montana, Idaho and South Carolina.

2 States have more than 50% enrollment in gold plans: New Mexico and Wyoming.

In New Jersey, more than 80% of plans are silver level plans; in Massachusetts, Mississippi and Alabama, more than 75% are.

Is this data indicative?

At first glance, it seems to indicate that most Americans must choose a lower premium plan regardless of risk: because platinum plans have the highest monthly premiums of any plan category but pay the most when medical care is needed, they may work well if there is the expectation for a great deal of health care and the consumer would rather pay a higher premium and know nearly all other costs are covered. Conversely, bronze plans expose a consumer to risk.

Yet platinum plans are not offered in every zip code of the United States. In fact, in many zip codes, silver level plans are the highest plans available for purchase.

In examining the data, it is possible to understand that consumers are not given a choice of plans by the insurance companies, who would prefer the consumer shoulder the risks of healthcare expenses. There may be many consumers who want platinum or gold plans who simply cannot purchase them.

Yet there may be another explanation when it is considered that because of the low overall enrollment and high costs, insurers in most areas have stopped offering platinum plans in the individual market: consumers may want the higher tier plans, but simply cannot afford them.

Are Bronze Plans Effective? What is Included in Preventive Care Benefits for Adults

All Marketplace health plans, regardless of metal tiers, must cover the following list of preventive services without charging you a copayment or coinsurance. This is true even if you haven't met your yearly deductible.

Ideally a bronze plan will provide all the costs of preventive services a healthy person needs.

If you are getting insurance for these preventative services only, you do not need to pay extra for them.

But what you won't see on this list is a checkup! Checkups are good to do, but are not covered as included preventative care and you will need to pay a copay or the cost of a regular doctor's visit for it. So, some cheaper plans will give you a handful of these sorts of visits for that purpose.

Those choosing cheaper, high deductible plans with no copays will usually find their monthly premium savings more than covers the cost of a checkup, though.

- Abdominal aortic aneurysm one-time screening for men of specified ages who have ever smoked
- Alcohol misuse screening and counseling
- Aspirin use to prevent cardiovascular disease and colorectal cancer for adults 50 to 59 years with a high cardiovascular risk
- Blood pressure screening
- Cholesterol screening for adults of certain ages or at higher risk
- Colorectal cancer screening for adults 45 to 75
- Depression screening
- Diabetes (Type 2) screening for adults 40 to 70 years who are overweight or obese

- Diet counseling for adults at higher risk for chronic disease
- Falls prevention (with exercise or physical therapy and vitamin D use) for adults 65 years and over, living in a community setting
- Hepatitis B screening for people at high risk, including people from countries with 2% or more Hepatitis B prevalence, and U.S.-born people not vaccinated as infants and with at least one parent born in a region with 8% or more Hepatitis B prevalence,
- Hepatitis C screening for adults age 18 to 79 years
- HIV screening for everyone age 15 to 65, and other ages at increased risk
- PrEP (pre-exposure prophylaxis) HIV prevention medication for HIV-negative adults at high risk for getting HIV through sex or injection drug use
- Lung cancer screening for adults 50 to 80 at high risk for lung cancer because they're heavy smokers or have quit in the past 15 years
- Obesity screening and counseling
- Sexually transmitted infection (STI) prevention counseling for adults at higher risk
- Statin preventive medication for adults 40 to 75 at high risk
- Syphilis screening for adults at higher risk
- Tobacco use screening for all adults and cessation interventions for tobacco users
- Tuberculosis screening for certain adults without symptoms at high risk
- Immunizations for adults — doses, recommended ages, and recommended populations vary:

- ☐ Chickenpox (Varicella)
- ☐ Diphtheria
- ☐ Flu (influenza)
- ☐ Hepatitis A
- ☐ Hepatitis B
- ☐ Human Papillomavirus (HPV)
- ☐ Measles
- ☐ Meningococcal
- ☐ Mumps
- ☐ Whooping Cough (Pertussis)
- ☐ Pneumococcal
- ☐ Rubella
- ☐ Shingles
- ☐ Tetanus

<u>Special Preventative Care for Women</u>

All Marketplace health plans must cover the following list of preventive services for women without charging a copayment or coinsurance. This is true even if you haven't met your yearly deductible.

1. Breastfeeding support and counseling from trained providers, and access to breastfeeding supplies, for pregnant and nursing women
2. Birth control: Food and Drug Administration-approved contraceptive methods, sterilization procedures, and patient education and counseling, as prescribed by a health care provider for women with reproductive capacity (but not including abortifacient drugs). However, this does

not apply to health plans sponsored by certain exempt "religious employers."

3. Folic acid supplements for women who may become pregnant
4. Gestational diabetes screening for women 24 weeks pregnant (or later) and those at high risk of developing gestational diabetes
5. Gonorrhea screening for all women at higher risk
6. Hepatitis B screening for pregnant women at their first prenatal visit
7. Maternal depression screening for mothers at well-baby visits (PDF, 1.5 MB)
8. Preeclampsia prevention and screening for pregnant women with high blood pressure
9. Rh incompatibility screening for all pregnant women and follow-up testing for women at higher risk
10. Syphilis screening
11. Expanded tobacco intervention and counseling for pregnant tobacco users
12. Urinary tract or other infection screening
13. Bone density screening for all women over age 65 or women age 64 and younger that have gone through menopause
14. Breast cancer genetic test counseling (BRCA) for women at higher risk
15. Breast cancer mammography screenings
16. Every 2 years for women 50 and over
17. As recommended by a provider for women 40 to 49 or women at higher risk for breast cancer
18. Breast cancer chemoprevention counseling for women at higher risk

19. Cervical cancer screening
20. Pap test (also called a Pap smear) for women age 21 to 65
21. Chlamydia infection screening for younger women and other women at higher risk
22. Diabetes screening for women with a history of gestational diabetes who aren't currently pregnant and who haven't been diagnosed with type 2 diabetes before
23. Domestic and interpersonal violence screening and counseling for all women (though men are statistically equally likely to suffer this form of violence, only women have this covered as a preventative treatment)
24. Gonorrhea screening for all women at higher risk
25. HIV screening and counseling for everyone age 15 to 65, and other ages at increased risk
26. PrEP (pre-exposure prophylaxis) HIV prevention medication for HIV-negative women at high risk for getting HIV through sex or injection drug use
27. Sexually transmitted infections counseling for sexually active women
28. Tobacco use screening and interventions
29. Urinary incontinence screening for women yearly
30. Well-woman visits to get recommended services for all women
31. Preventive care benefits for children

Special Preventative Care for Children

Most health plans must cover a set of preventive health services for children at no cost, no matter what metal tier is selected, without a copayment or coinsurance. This is true even if you haven't met your yearly deductible.

1. Alcohol, tobacco, and drug use assessments for adolescents
2. Autism screening for children at 18 and 24 months
3. Behavioral assessments for children: Age 0 to 11 months, 1 to 4 years, 5 to 10 years, 11 to 14 years, 15 to 17 years
4. Bilirubin concentration screening for newborns
5. Blood pressure screening for children: Age 0 to 11 months, 1 to 4 years , 5 to 10 years, 11 to 14 years, 15 to 17 years
6. Blood screening for newborns
7. Depression screening for adolescents beginning routinely at age 12
8. Developmental screening for children under age 3
9. Dyslipidemia screening for all children once between 9 and 11 years and once between 17 and 21 years, and for children at higher risk of lipid disorders
10. Fluoride supplements for children without fluoride in their water source
11. Fluoride varnish for all infants and children as soon as teeth are present
12. Gonorrhea preventive medication for the eyes of all newborns
13. Hearing screening for all newborns; and regular screenings for children and adolescents as recommended by their provider
14. Height, weight and body mass index (BMI) measurements taken regularly for all children
15. Hematocrit or hemoglobin screening for all children
16. Hemoglobinopathies or sickle cell screening for newborns
17. Hepatitis B screening for adolescents at higher risk

18. Hypothyroidism screening for newborns
19. PrEP (pre-exposure prophylaxis) HIV prevention medication for HIV-negative adolescents at high risk for getting HIV through sex or injection drug use
20. Lead screening for children at risk of exposure
21. Obesity screening and counseling
22. Oral health risk assessment (PDF, 609 KB) for young children from 6 months to 6 years
23. Phenylketonuria (PKU) screening for newborns
24. Sexually transmitted infection (STI) prevention counseling and screening for adolescents at higher risk
25. Tuberculin testing for children at higher risk of tuberculosis: Age 0 to 11 months, 1 to 4 years, 5 to 10 years, 11 to 14 years, 15 to 17 years
26. Vision screening for all children
27. Well-baby and well-child visits
28. Immunizations for children from birth to age 18 — doses, recommended ages, and recommended populations vary:
   - Chickenpox (Varicella)
   - Diphtheria, tetanus, and pertussis (DTaP)
   - Haemophilus influenza type b
   - Hepatitis A
   - Hepatitis B
   - Human Papillomavirus (HPV)
   - Inactivated Poliovirus
   - Influenza (flu shot)
   - Measles
   - Meningococcal
   - Mumps
   - Pneumococcal
   - Rubella

- Rotavirus

Understanding Insurance Terms: Deductible, Copays, Coinsurance, and Out of Pocket Maximums

The various products of health insurance differ in regard to their deductible, co-pay, co-insurance and out of pocket maximums. Let's understand these terms and what they mean in shopping.

Deductibles

Deductibles quantify the risk you are assuming when you purchase the insurance: beneath this threshold, you are responsible for every dollar of cost - except where co-pays are agreed upon.

This is why the pre-deductible expenses are called the "gap." Make sure the gap is not bigger than you can step over comfortably: whether by payment plans to the doctor, or to the bank or credit card company, you will have to pay this amount. Plans with larger deductibles are typically cheaper: some consumers will take the savings in premium and set it aside for future deductibles. But though it is wise to do so, most consumers lack this discipline and do not do save the difference.

Insurance typically offers some benefit for its owner in this pre-deductible risk: insurance companies are able to negotiate lower costs of service from providers, and frequently offer services to reduce risks of owners (to improve their health - such as discounted gym membership, or preventative care). Sometimes, some services are available through a copay (such as $40 to see your primary care doctor).

But HSA's offer more, in the form of tax benefits. Owners of HSA's may use pre-tax dollars to pay for their deductible - and all other medical expenses.

And EPO's offer a contracted rate of service that is frequently cheaper than what is available elsewhere.

It is important to understand that deductibles are measured by calendar years: so, typically between January 1 and December 31. If you meet your deductible on December 30, and have another medical expense on January 2, that expense would apply to the next year's deductible. Which is why elective medical procedures are typically undertaken before the end of the year - or at the beginning of it. And a reason why some families might even opt to induce labor early, since a December baby is typically cheaper than a January baby, given the amount of money spent on medicine and care for the mother until that point.

It bears mentioning too, that a child is born into their mother's plan, and normal birth costs apply to her deductible. However, the child must get their own plan within 30 days, and if they require treatment or services, it will apply to their own deductible. This said, in Colorado, most children will qualify for CHP+, a form of medicaid insurance.

Plans typically have both an individual and family deductible: when the family deductible is met, any other member of that family has their deductible met.

Co-pays

Co-pays are the payments made by the owner of the policy in addition to what the insurance company will pay: in the insurance agreement, the insurance company typically agrees to pay the bulk of the expense for some routine medical expenses.

So, for example, if you can see your primary care doctor with a $20 copay, this means that the insurance company is actually paying the doctor's bill - except for the $20 you agree to pay for. If you can get a prescription for a $5 copay, you are agreeing to pay $5 and the insurance company is agreeing to pay the rest.

Consumers are typically responsible for these co-pays even after reaching their out of pocket maximums.

Some plans do not have copay agreements. HSA's typically do not. Bronze plans sometimes don't, or severely limit the obligations of the insurance company to a certain number of purchases or service provisions. But some plans offer generous co-pays. Typically for more premium expense.

Co-pays can save you a lot of money - but only if you use them a lot, typically for chronic diseases. Do you regularly visit doctors or regularly get expensive medicines? Calculate the potential savings by: subtracting the greater premium expense of a more costly plan with lower copays from the higher cost of services and medicine without copays on a cheaper plan.

Co-insurance

Co-insurance is similar to a co-payment, in that it represents the agreement between the policy owner and the insurance company to split costs after the deductible is met.

So, if a policy comes with 80% coinsurance, this means that the insurance company will pay 80 cents, or 80%, of every dollar of costs after the deductible is met, and the policy owner will pay 20 cents, or 20%.

This is subject to coverage limitations: just because a policy owner may purchase acupuncture services, or lasik surgery, does not mean that their insurance policy covers these things: dollars paid for uncovered services do not count toward the deductible, and are not subjected to the agreements of coinsurance or copayments.

Additional coverage limitations may exist, such as costs for healthcare resulting from illegal activities: if a person is breaking the law, and gets hurt doing so, the insurance will not likely cover that healthcare.

But there are limits that work in favor of the consumer as well: these are called "out of pocket maximums"

Out of pocket and coverage maximums

The out of pocket maximum is the most that a policy owner will have to pay for healthcare costs: the insurance company agrees to cover everything after that amount. Except, usually, co-pays.

It is similar in this regard to a policy coverage maximum, where the policy owner agrees to pay for everything after a coverage maximum. However, most plans do not have coverage maximums anymore.

Maternity is a condition unlike most others - especially from an insurance agent's perspective. That's because the patient knows far in advance that they will be having a very large expense which may even exceed their out of pocket maximum for any given policy - and that they will be adding a newborn to that policy who has a statistically high chance of meeting the out of pocket maximum for the policy too.

Plans typically have both an individual and family maximum out of pockets: when the family maximum out of pocket is met, any other member of that family has their out of pocket maximum met.

Practice examples

If a person were to go see their primary care physician for a tight chest, and learn that they need to immediately go to the hospital for emergency treatment that costs $20,000, and owns a policy that has:

- $20 copay for visiting a primary care physician
- $500 copay for emergency room visits
- $2000 deductible
- 80% coinsurance
- $6000 out of pocket maximum

How much would the policy owner pay?

- $20 for visiting the primary care physician
- $500 for visiting the emergency room
- $2000 deductible

=====================

= $2520

This leaves $18,000 left to be covered: copays don't get applied to the deductible.

$18,000 x 20% coinsurance = $3600 owed for treatment
$3600 coinsurance + $2520 copays and deductible = $6120

This is $120 over the maximum out of pocket... so the policy owner will only pay $6000. Should they need another emergency visit later that year, the insurance would pay for it entirely.

This said, some policies make copays not subject to the deductible or out of pocket maximum, in which case you always have to pay them.

Beyond Metal Plans: Plans of the Past and Future

At first, it may seem that the choice of metal plans comes down to your own preference for risk. Yet, the choice of what insurance plan you select is sometimes limited by what plans are available in your area. However, it is more accurate to say that the decision is limited by your ability to afford to reduce your risks of healthcare expenses: no one wants to be responsible for the risk of enormous emergency expenses, but few can become responsible for enormous premium costs they will pay regardless of an emergency procedure.

In the past, before metal plans, there existed several products - and these are becoming increasingly relevant in a post-metal world as well.

Gap Plans

From this quandary has arisen alternative insurance products to health insurance, intended to literally fill the gap created by high deductible plans.

This has sometimes taken the form of "gap" plans which cover the costs of deductibles incurred. However, because the cost of these "gap" plans is usually equivalent to the difference in premium between a bronze and silver level plan, there is little incentive for a consumer to purchase it - unless they learn, mid way through their deductible year, that they face a higher risk of medical costs.

Indemnity Plans

But it has also taken the form of indemnity plans.
There are a wide variety of indemnity plans.

Medical indemnity plans aren't like regular insurance and don't have to conform to ACA requirements, so they can exclude preexisting conditions, as well as a variety of other conditions as well.

Some will be triggered by an emergency event, in which case the insurance company pays out a predetermined amount of money to you in the event of an injury, hospitalizing sickness or critical illness: typical coverage levels might be $5,000, or $10,000, or even as low as $500. This money not only offsets the costs of healthcare, but theoretically may soften the loss of working hours from the injury or sickness in the first place.

Some indemnity plans are of a fee-for-service type: you can use any medical provider (such as a doctor and hospital). You or the provider sends the bill to the insurance company, which pays part of it. Usually, you have a deductible—such as $200—to pay each year before the insurer starts paying.

Once you meet the deductible, most of these sorts of indemnity plans pay a percentage of what they consider the "Usual and Customary" charge for covered services - which may or may not be what you were charged. The insurer generally pays 80 percent of the "Usual and Customary" costs and you pay the other 20 percent, which is known as coinsurance. If the provider charges more than the "Usual and Customary" rates, you will have to pay both the coinsurance and the difference.

The plan will pay for charges for medical tests and prescriptions as well as from doctors and hospitals. It may not pay for some preventive care, like checkups.

Life Insurance

Life insurance is not only for the dead, but also for the dying - and the "I'm fine and quite alive thank you" consumer as well.

There are several forms of life insurance which help out in medical emergencies. Some plans allow the build up of cash value over time, which can be used for medical purposes in a process called acceleration that effectively allows a person to draw funds against the death benefit in advance of death to (hopefully) prevent death from happening.

In order to accelerate your life insurance death benefit, you need to be diagnosed with a qualifying medical condition - and not all medical conditions apply. Different carriers have a list of different conditions that can qualify you to use your living benefits. Some of the most common ones are a heart attack, stroke or cancer.

Then, you would need to file a claim with the life insurance carrier. The company will provide you with the forms you need to complete and request a copy of your medical records. Once they receive the claim package, they will review the information and assess the severity and your life expectancy. Afterward, based on the information provided, they will make you an offer. You have the option of accepting or rejecting the offer.

With permanent life insurance, premiums paid into the policy can sometimes be pulled out to pay for medical costs. Whatever money you take out, however, will reduce the policy's values and death benefit and possibly create adverse income tax consequences. If you have permanent life insurance and have built up cash in the policy, you may have the ability to access those funds to pay for medical bills. Like all loans, you will need to repay the insurance company with interest. Otherwise, your policy can lapse, or your beneficiaries can receive a lower death benefit than you initially intended. However, unlike taking a loan from a bank or other lender, the loan is not dependent on credit checks and may offer better interest rates.

And in many cases, if you become permanently disabled, you can ask for a waiver of premium, and funnel that money you'd be spending every month toward medical costs. Other policies have long term care riders that allow you to use the benefits for long term care facilities and costs.

A Simple Choice, After All

In the end, the choice for insurance is a simple one: it is a needed product. The costs of healthcare without it are disastrous. Even if that disaster permits you to end up on Medicaid, there is a chance that you may not receive the care from the doctors or facilities you want (who do not take Medicaid), or that the costs that were incurred on your way toward qualifying for Medicaid cannot easily be recovered from.

The reasonable desire to not become overinsured does encourage a consumer toward bronze plans. As does financial limitations that prevent purchasing higher tier plans. Or limits placed upon the market by insurers who will not offer higher tier plans. However, the desire for greater coverage is always motivated by the extraordinary costs of hospitals, doctors and medicine.

While reasonable legislative reform may one day control these costs, there exists a real potential for insurance companies - and their consumers - to pressure medical costs downward. Not by refusing to obtain service, but by insisting on fair, usual and customary costs.

But until then, the choice for what insurance to obtain will come down to what can be afforded: with subsidies and cost reduction programs, many higher level plans become obtainable for the average consumer. And we have seen real data confirming a mutual preference - by consumers and insurance companies - for silver plans, and secondarily, bronze plans.

Yet it may be in fact that the future solution lies in the past, and through indemnity plans, life insurance and gap plans, the consumer may obtain the flexibility needed to navigate the increasingly complex world of American healthcare where the question of what insurance will you choose and why is less important than if you will have any regrets for your decision in the future.